Specials!

Textiles

Josie Brown and Julie Messenger

Acknowledgements

© 2007 Folens Limited, on behalf of the authors.

United Kingdom: Folens Publishers, Apex Business Centre, Boscombe Road, Dunstable, LU5 4RL.
www.folens@folens.com

Ireland: Folens Publishers, Greenhills Road, Tallaght, Dublin 24.
Email: info@folens.ie

Editor: Saskia Gwinn   Layout artists: Book Matrix

Illustrations: J.B. Illustrations   Cover design: Holbrook Design

Cover image: Corbis

First published 2007 by Folens Limited.

Every effort has been made to contact copyright holders of material used in this publication. If any copyright holder has been overlooked, we should be pleased to make any necessary arrangements.

British Library Cataloguing in Publication Data. A catalogue record for this publication is available from the British Library.

ISBN 978 1 85008 231 6

Contents

Introduction

Specials! D&T is divided into ten units. A unit has one or more photocopiable resource sheets and several activity sheets. This allows the teacher to work in different ways. For example, the unit could be taught as a lesson with students in groups of varying sizes. Alternatively, a single resource sheet and its related activity sheets could be used as support material. The Teacher's notes give guidance and are laid out as follows:

Objectives

These are the main skills or knowledge to be learned.

Prior knowledge

This refers to the minimum skills or knowledge required by the students to complete the tasks. As a rule, students should have a reading comprehension age of 7 to 9 years and should be working at levels 1 to 3. Some student pages are more challenging than others and you will need to select accordingly.

QCA and NC links, Scottish attainment targets, Northern Ireland and Wales links

All units link to the QCA Scheme of Work and the NC for D&T at key stage 3 and the Scottish attainment targets. Where relevant, these are also links to the programmes of study in Northern Ireland and Wales.

Background

This gives additional information for the teacher, expanding on or giving further information about this unit.

Starter activity

Since the units can be taught as a lesson, a warm-up activity, focusing on an aspect of the unit, is suggested.

Resource and activity sheets

The resource sheet, which is often visual, but may also be written, does not usually include tasks and can be used as a stimulus for discussion. Related tasks are provided on activity sheets. Where necessary, keywords are included on the student pages. Other keywords are included within the Teacher's notes. These can be introduced to students at the teacher's discretion and depending on the students' ability.

Plenary

The teacher can use the suggestions here to recap on the main points covered or to reinforce a particular idea. Work related to assessment, ICT or other media may also be suggested.

Assessment sheet

At the end of each unit, students can use the assessment sheet to assess their own progress. The teacher should add a simple checklist of between three and seven points relating to the D&T curriculum covered in each unit. Students can subsequently set targets to achieve according to their performance.

Teacher's notes

How fibres and fabrics are made

Objectives

- To know whether a fibre is from a natural source or is manufactured
- To be able to distinguish between plant and animal sources
- To understand the processes of weaving, knitting and felting
- To understand and to use terms such as strength, stretch, felting and so on relation to fabrics
- (For the teacher) To begin to see how much experience of using textiles individual students have had

Prior knowledge

At the start of Key Stage 3, the students will have had different experiences of textile projects; they could be asked to complete a simple form to indicate their previous experiences.

QCA links

Unit 7aiii Understanding materials Focus: textiles

NC links

KS 3 Scheme of work – Unit 8B Wallets

Scottish attainment targets

Environmental Studies – Technology – Knowledge & Understanding
Strand – Resources and how they are managed
Level D, Level E

Wales links

3.1   3.2

Northern Ireland links

Knowledge and understanding – Manufacturing materials, components, techniques & processes

Background

A fabric is made from fibres. There are many different fibres available and there are different ways of making them into fabrics. The focus of this unit is to distinguish natural from manufactured fibres and to look at how fabrics can be made.

Starter activity

Teachers should provide students with as large a selection of fibres as possible for them to handle and talk about. The students should focus their discussion on the sources of the fibres, including references to their texture and properties. When the fibres have been examined, show the students, and let them handle, woven knitted and bonded fabrics (such as interfacing).

Resource and activity sheets

The resource sheet 'How fibres and fabrics are made' focuses on some basic key terms.

The activity sheet 'Natural and manufactured fibres' depicts plant, animal and manufactured sources and fibres. Ask students to match up the plants, animals and manufactured sources to the finished products. Draw out that the reason for this exercise is to distinguish manufactured and natural fibres. Supply a selection of fabrics from which students should select four examples of cotton, woollen, nylon and polyester. Ask the students to name each example.

The activity sheet 'Looms and weaving' enables students to experience weaving, whilst also reinforcing some of the terms found on the resource sheet 'How fibres and fabrics are made.' The students will need a box to use as a loom – the lid off a box of photocopier paper is ideal – and a selection of materials to weave with.

'Knitted textiles' helps the students to explore knitted fabrics. Students should work in pairs and follow the instructions to unravel a knitted fabric identifying the loops, which are locked together when fibres are knitted. Prompts are provided to help students to look at the stretchiness of knitted fabrics and to record their own sets of results.

The activity sheet 'Bonded and felted fabrics' encourages students to look at bonded fabrics. They will need to experience samples of both natural (felt) and synthetic (interfacing) fabrics. Introduce students to the key terms provided. To conclude this activity they should use the activity sheet to design and make an item, which relies on the non-fraying characteristics of felt.

Plenary

Encourage students to identify fabrics and their component fibres in the everyday world around them. Introduce the concept that the convenience, cheapness and attractiveness of a fabric may, for some users, be more important than strength and durability.

How fibres and fabrics are made

Fibre

These are the small hairs that a fabric is made of. They can be from plants, animals, or be made from chemicals.

Yarn

Fibres are made into threads, which are called yarn.

Fabric or material

Yarn and fibres are made into sheets from which products are made.

Textile

This is a knitted, woven or bonded fabric.

Woven

Yarn is stretched lengthwise on a frame called a loom (this is the **warp**). It is interlaced with another set of threads (the **weft**). A fabric made like this is woven.

Knitted

If the fabric is made of one inter-looped thread, it is **knitted**.

Felted or bonded

Wool is a natural fibre; it can be matted to make sheets of fabric. Made fibres can be bonded into sheets by heating, pressing or gluing them.

Strength

How well are the fibres held together? A material can be strong or weak. This affects its use.

Fray

An unfinished (**raw**) edge of a woven fabric can undo or fray.

Right Side

Sometimes the two sides of a fabric look different. The best side is called the **Right Side** and is the one we want to see.

Natural and manufactured fibres

Fibres are the hairs that are put together to make a fabric.

Natural fibres come from animals or plants. **Manufactured** or **made** fibres may come from coal or oil, or they can be waste fibres, which are bonded together with a chemical.

☞ Draw lines to join the source of the fibres on the left to the finished product on the right.

Source of fibre	Finished product

☞ Write **natural** or **manufactured** under each fabric source.

☞ Choose four pieces of fabric and staple them onto the back of this sheet. Write down their names. You should choose some natural and some manufactured fabrics.

Looms and weaving

☞ Study the stages below which show you how to weave. Your teacher will help you to try weaving.

To help you to weave, you will need:

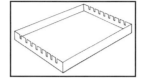

- a box with slots cut into it like this:

- yarn to be the **warp** threads   • wool   • strips of fabric

- lace or paper as **weft** threads to weave in and out.

These drawings and instructions show you what you should do:

1. Put wool or string on the loom. These are **warp** threads.	
2. Use wool or strips of fabric as **weft** threads. A large needle will help.	
3. To change a **weft** thread, leave some of it hanging at the side.	
4. Lift your work off the loom.	
5. Turn any long pieces under and glue or staple them so that they don't become undone.	

Activity sheet – How fibres and fabrics are made

Knitted textiles

☞ Work with a partner to help you to fill in the table below.

You will need:

- a piece of knitted fabric
- a magnifying glass to see the loops
- a ruler to measure the stretch.

☞ Now, follow each of the steps in the table. **Your teacher will help you**.

What you must do	Write or draw what you see
Find a thread and pull it. It will undo. Look at the loops as they undo. They were made with needles. Draw the loops.	
Look at the fabric. Are its two sides the same?	
Look at the thread you have pulled. Is it curly or straight? Draw it.	
Is the fabric natural or manmade?	
What was this fabric for?	
Measure one of the sides of your fabric. Do not pull it as you measure. Now pull it and measure it again. If measurement 2 was longer than measurement 1, your fabric was stretchy.	Measurement 1: Measurement 2:

Bonded and felted fabrics

☞ Use **felt** to make a bookmark. First you should note these things:

- both sides of felt look the same
- it does not **fray** when it is cut
- it is a weak fabric and you can pull it apart.

☞ Now, design a bookmark.

1. Use the rectangle as the pattern (or template) for your bookmark.
2. Write your name or initials on coloured paper. Use big letters or bubble writing. Cut them out to use them as a pattern for your letters.
3. Cut out more shapes if you wish. Arrange them on the rectangle in different ways.
4. When you have decided on your best design, use the patterns to cut the letters, shapes and rectangle out of felt.
5. Fix the parts on with glue or sew them on.

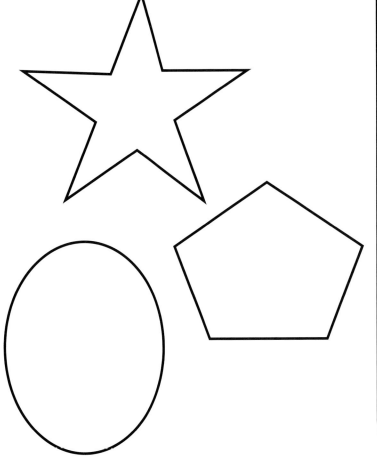

Textiles

Teacher's notes

Properties of fabrics

Objectives

- To understand the term **property**
- To be able to match a property to a product's purpose
- To be able to identify what properties a simple product needs and to make such a product
- To be able to sort fabrics according to their properties
- To evaluate a range of products according to their suitability for a purpose

Prior knowledge

Students need to understand what a fabric is and to have experienced sorting and matching activities. They should think about fabrics and products which are not present in the classroom.

QCA links

Unit 7iii Understanding materials Focus: textiles
Unit 8biii Designing for clients Focus: textiles

NC links

KS3 Scheme of work – Unit 8B Wallets

Scottish attainment targets

Environmental Studies – Technology – Knowledge & Understanding: Strand – Resources and how they are managed: Level E
Strand – Needs and how they are met: Level D
Strand – Processes and how they are applied: Level C
Environmental Studies – Skills in Technology – designing and making: Strand – Preparing for tasks: Level D

Wales links

3.1   3.2

Northern Ireland links

Knowledge and understanding – Manufacturing materials, components, techniques and processes

Background

This unit focuses on the effect that a property, such as absorbency, will have on a product's fitness for a purpose. Drawings have been provided. Other activities require the actual provision of articles for the children to handle and discuss. The **properties** of any fabric determine how suitable for a given purpose it will be. In order to convey an understanding of **properties** to students, this unit will focus on a few simple properties.

Starter activity

Students should be encouraged to contribute to a class brain storm. A product should be chosen by the teacher, for example, a motor cycle helmet. Students should suggest what properties it must have and to write these down.

Resource and activity sheets

The resource sheet 'Properties of fabrics' defines and compares some basic properties of materials.

The activity sheet 'What's this fabric like?' depicts the properties of different materials, which the students should match to a list of products. Explain to students that not all of the products are textiles, because the word **property** applies to all materials.

When working on activity sheet 'Looking at fabric' provide students with samples of materials, which they should examine. Students should use the word bank to help them to describe and name each of the materials in the boxes. It may be necessary to edit the word bank to suit their needs.

Whilst using the activity sheet 'Design a cushion fit for its purpose' students should decide what the purpose of the cushion will be, for example, they might wish to design a floor cushion or a scatter cushion. They should then identify the properties that a material will need from which to make their cushion so that it is fit for its purpose. Samples of fabrics and fillings should also be made available to students. The students may not be ready to choose the filling for their product, give guidance here. They will find it easier to develop ideas if they work in small groups.

The activity sheet 'Comparing products' encourages students to look at existing products and to evaluate them according to their purposes. Students should be provided with a range of containers from plastic bags and tins to products manufactured to cater for a specific purpose. They should complete the table. Encourage students to use the key terms: **fabric strength**, **durability**, **cost**, **fit for purpose**, **attractiveness** and **fastenings.**

Plenary

Encourage discussion about products in general terms.

Properties of fabrics

Absorbent

A fabric which soaks up (absorbs) liquids. Kitchen towel is absorbent.

Waterproof

A fabric that keeps water out.

Warm

This provides **insulation** and lets less heat in or out.

Cool

This is a fabric that keeps us from getting too hot. It is often a natural fibre like cotton. It allows sweat to get out and to evaporate. It lets the air get in and out.

Flammable

This is a fabric that can catch fire.

Flame proof

This is a fabric that does not catch fire easily. Sometimes **flammable** fabrics are treated with a **fire retardant** (a chemical which makes it harder for them to burn) on them. To make them safer, beds and sofas have fire retardants.

Durable

This means that a fabric will last well. Some materials must be strong to work well or be **fit for purpose**. Shoes need to be durable.

Texture

This is how something feels. Fabrics may feel smooth like silk or rough, for example, the soles of shoes should be rough to grip well.

Textiles

Activity sheet – Properties of fabrics

What's this fabric like?

☞ Here is a list of properties of different materials.

Draw lines to match the properties to the products. An example has been given.

jumpers	**absorbent**	sports clothes
motor cycle leathers	**waterproof**	towel
t-shirt	**cool**	shorts
kitchen towel	**breathable**	fireman's coat
cotton wool	**warm**	umbrella
pyjamas	**flame proof**	gloves
plastic sheet	**durable**	silk tie
out-door jackets	**soft**	denim jeans
	high visibility	
	reflective	

Looking at fabrics

☞ This activity will tell you how some fabrics look and feel.

You should use the resource sheet 'Properties of fabrics' to help you.

Your teacher will give you some fabrics to look at. Write the name of each fabric in the left column. Choose words from the word bank to help you to fill in the column on the right.

Word bank
stiff   flimsy   strong   weak   lasting   soft to touch   rough to touch   patterned   plain

Fabric name	**How does the fabric look and feel?**

Activity sheet – Properties of fabrics

Design a cushion fit for its purpose

☞ You are going to choose a fabric to make a cushion. Decide how it will be used and who will use it by filling in the table below.

Think about these things	Words to help you to think	Write your choices here
What sort of cushion will it be?	floor cushion, chair cushion and pillow.	
Who will use it?	my friends and I, my family, visitors and my grandmother.	
How will they use it?	to sit on, for comfort, to look nice and as a pillow.	
What are the properties of the fabric you will use?	soft, flame proof, warm or cool and durable, waterproof and breathable.	
What type of fabric will you use?	plain, patterned, fleecy cotton, synthetic, leather and easy to wash.	
What will the size and shape of the cushion be?	square, rectangle and round. 45cm 30cm 20cm.	
What will you put into it?	polyester fibre and polyester beads.	

Comparing products

A product is something made for a purpose. Different products can fulfil the same purpose. For example, there is more than one way to store pencils.

☞ Look at containers for pencils provided by your teacher. Write your views about them in the table below.

The column called 'How many stars?' can be used to record your feelings about the product.

The blank rows are for you to add other pencil containers that you might look at.

Type of container	What is it made of?	Is it fit for its purpose?	Will it last? (Durability)	How many stars? *****
Plastic bag				
Tin box				
Fabric pencil case				
Plastic pencil case				

☞ Which container did you like the most?

The container I liked the most was...I liked it because.......

Teacher's notes

Textile products

Objectives

- To think about the role of textiles in keeping us healthy and safe
- To understand that the properties of a fabric determine what it can be used for
- To understand that it is necessary to think about the purpose of a product when choosing the materials that will be used
- To know that special processes during the manufacture of some fabrics will make them reflective, strong, waterproof and so on

Prior knowledge

Students should have learned about knitted and woven fabrics during their work in 'How fibres and fabrics are made' and will understand what is referred to by a **fabric's properties**. The use of adhesives may be necessary to help students to achieve a satisfactory end product. It will also be helpful if the students have learned about reflected light in science lessons.

QCA links

Unit 8iii Designing for clients Focus: textiles
Unit 9aiii Selecting materials Focus: textiles

NC links

KS3 Scheme of work – Unit 7A Be seen!

Scottish attainment targets

Environmental Studies – Technology – Knowledge & Understanding: Strand – Resources and how they are managed: Level E
Strand – Processes and how they are applied: Level D
Environmental Studies – Skills in Technology – designing and making: Strand – Preparing for tasks: Level D

Wales links

3.1   3.2

Northern Ireland links

Knowledge and understanding – Manufacturing materials, components, techniques and processes

Background

This unit will help students to appreciate that textiles are everywhere and fulfil many purposes. It is difficult to provide a wide range of technical fabrics for

students to examine, but they can still be discussed and examples can be found in the everyday world.

Starter activity

Help students to understand that a textile needs to fulfil a purpose by asking them to list the textiles products they can see in the classroom. They should be encouraged to say what qualities the textiles are demonstrating, for example, hardwearing, soft and comfortable, easy to see, attractive and so on. Ask them to think about which attributes of the textile were added during the manufacturing process.

Resource and activity sheets

The resource sheet 'Textiles to keep us safe' seeks to illustrate the wide range of textiles found in the modern world. It should also prompt early discussion of special manmade fabrics.

The activity sheet 'Textiles around us' asks students to identify textiles that are reflective, used for safety and for insulation, for sports purposes, as well as textiles which are used in the everyday environment.

The activity sheet 'Make a reflective zipper tag' allows students to design and make a reflective badge. Students will require a range of Day-Glo and reflective materials. It is important that they understand what **reflective** means and that this property is a result of how the fabric is made. Provide students with mirrors and torches so that they can experience reflecting light in pairs. Explain to students the keywords: **reflective**, **bright** and **visibility**. When students are ready to design their badge, enlarge the base template provided. Students should then follow the instructions to make the zipper tag.

'Keep a water bottle cool' focuses on fabrics that can be used to keep something from losing or gaining heat. Students should follow the instructions to make a bottle cover; the article made can be a padded container for a drinks bottle (as described on the activity sheet) or for a lunch box. Explain keywords to students.

The activity sheet 'Ear defenders' focuses on safety clothing. The students are asked to make and test ear defenders. A selection of ear defenders should be provided for them to try out. When trying out the ear defenders, a bell or a buzzer is necessary to make the sound a constant.

Plenary

The students could be asked to consider **smart** textiles and to imagine a situation in which a textile's properties can remedy a health and safety issue. Allow them to sketch ideas.

Textiles to keep us safe

☞ Read these fabric descriptions.

Reflective fabrics contain thousands and thousands of tiny glass beads that act like mirrors.

Fluorescent and **Day-Glo** describe colourful fabrics.

High visibility means the fabric is easy to see.

Textiles around us

Textiles have lots of uses in our daily lives. Sometimes it is easy to see them, for example, as clothes and on furniture. They are used in buildings, but it is sometimes hard to see them. Textiles help us to stay safe everyday, for example, seat belts in cars. Clothing may keep us safe at work, during sport, whilst travelling or at home. Some examples of textiles in our lives are drawn below.

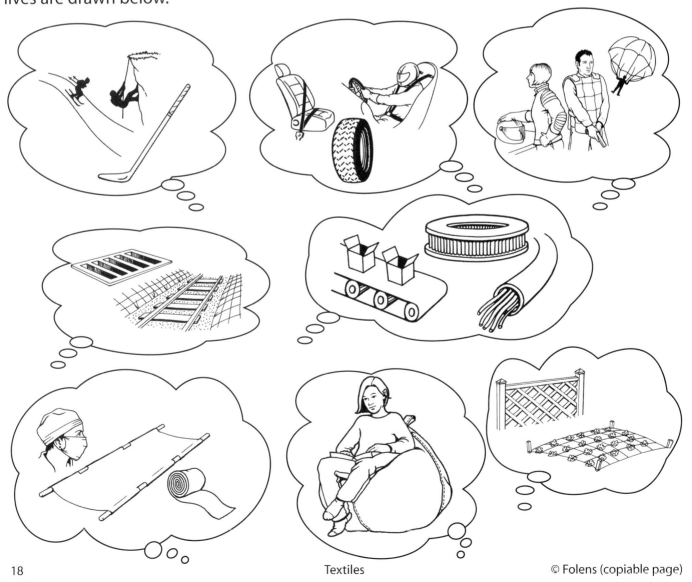

Activity sheet – Textile products

Textiles around us

☞ In this table, list the textile products that you can see on the resource sheet, 'Textiles to keep us safe'.

Write a name or draw a picture in each of the spaces. Each space is labelled with a product use.

You could add more headings if you need them on the back of this sheet.

Reflective products	Protection in the home
Keeping things hot or cold	**Protection outside the home**
Sports products	**Protection at work**
Furnishings	**Everyday life**

Make a reflective zipper tag

☞ Use this sheet to make a reflective zipper tag. First carry out these tasks.

You will need:

a mirror, a torch, pieces of **reflective** fabric, some brightly coloured (Day-Glo) and **fluorescent** fabrics.

1. Look at the fabrics in daylight. Talk to a partner about how easy they are to see. This is **visibility**.

2. Now, take the same samples somewhere darker and talk about their **visibility** again.

3. Take turns to shine the torch onto the mirror and watch the **reflected** light bounce off. Shine the torch onto the pieces of fabric.

    Is the **visibility** of **brightly coloured** and **reflective** materials different?

☞ You have looked at bright and reflective materials.

Now make a reflective zipper tag:

1. Use the shape below as a pattern (or template) for your tag. Draw some simple shapes to put on your tag.

2. Cut out two of each shape and two bases.

3. Fix them together.

4. Use a hole punch to make a hole and attach the badge to a zip.

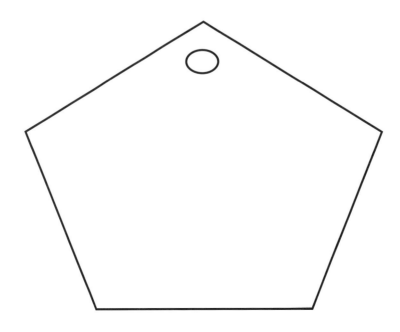

Activity sheet – Textile products

Keep a water bottle cool

Fabric can keep things warm or cool.

- Keeping it **cool** means keeping heat out.
- Keeping it **warm** means keeping heat in.

It needs fabric, which **insulates**. It slows down air movement to keep heat in or keep heat out.

☞ You can make a bottle cooler by following these steps:

1.	You will need a plastic bottle, polyester wadding (to **insulate**), pieces of fabric (for the cover) and some A4 paper.	
2.	Use a piece of paper to make a pattern for the bottle cover. Wrap a piece of paper around the bottle and allow 1cm extra. Cut out the pattern.	
3.	Cut out one piece of wadding and two pieces of fabric using the pattern.	
4.	Pin the wadding and the fabric together and sew along two sides with a zig-zag stitch.	
5.	Fold over and sew the top seam. Leave a gap to put a lace in.	
6.	Put the water bottle into the bag and pull the lace shut.	

☞ **Now test it!**

Using a thermometer, test the water every ten minutes.

Try this with the bottle in the bag and out of the bag.

Ear defenders

☞ A product which lowers **harmful** noises is an **ear defender**.

Look at manufactured **ear defenders**. Try them on and look at the part that goes over your ears. Answer these questions:

- Do they fit? Can you **adjust** them?
- Is the noise less? What keeps some noise out?
- How can you make your own?

Making your product

☞ Now, follow these steps to make your own ear defenders.

1. Use two strips of card and a stapler to make a frame.

2. Draw a shape to cover your ears. Check that it is the right size. Cut two of these shapes out of card.

3. Choose a fabric which will make noise less. Cut out two pieces and stick them on to the card.

4. They will not last without covers. Make covers and use glue or staples to fix them on.

5. Fix the ear defenders onto the frame.

Testing the ear defenders

☞ Now, use a bell or a buzzer – so that the noise is the same – to test each set of ear defenders.

Discuss what you found hard about this activity. What did you find easy?

Teacher's notes

Patterns and planning work with textiles

Objectives

- To understand what a pattern is
- To know what pattern markings and terms mean
- To make and use a simple pattern
- To produce a product by using a pattern and following simple instructions

Prior knowledge

The students need to be able to use simple tools, such as scissors, competently. They will also need to be able to use pins to join the pattern to the fabric and are expected to be able to follow basic written instructions.

QCA links

Unit 8iii Designing for clients Focus: textiles
Unit 9aiii Selecting materials Focus: textiles

NC links

KS3 Scheme of Work Unit 8B Wallets and Unit 8E Juggling balls and Unit 9E Designer bags

Scottish attainment targets

Environmental Studies – Technology – Knowledge & Understanding: Strand – Resources and how they are managed: Level C
Environmental Studies – Skills in Technology – designing and making: Strand – Preparing for tasks: Level D
Strand – Carrying out tasks: Level D
Strand – Reviewing and reporting on tasks: Level D

Wales links

3.2

Northern Ireland links

Knowledge & understanding – Designing as an imaginative and creative activity which brings together knowledge and understanding of communication, techniques, materials & components

Background

A pattern is essentially a model of the parts of a product drawn on paper. Students need to understand the conventions they will meet when they use a pattern. This unit focuses on the use of patterns to produce a product. It helps students to understand how to use a pattern, also providing practical experience through making a container.

Resource and activity sheets

The basic conventional markings found on patterns are reproduced on the resource sheet 'Terms and symbols used on patterns' and can be kept by students for reference. Discuss what a **pattern** is and explore the students' understanding of seam allowances, the grain of the fabric and so on. Follow on with activity sheet 'Pattern markings', which is an exercise that can be used to reinforce students' understanding of pattern markings.

Using their knowledge of patterns, ask students to complete activity sheet 'A pattern to make a glove puppet'. Students should follow the instructions provided. How they decorate the finished puppet is optional; you may wish to expand their options to include using beads, buttons and so on. This activity aims to encourage the correct use of a pattern, inserting pins and accurate cutting out. Enlarge the pattern provided at the bottom of the sheet to help students. Test the size of the pattern by placing a hand on it. In order to make the puppet, the student's hand must fit inside the stitching line with a space of at least 1.5cm all around it.

Activity sheet 'Make and use a pattern 1: pencil case' asks students to identify the skills they will need to learn in order to make a pencil case. They are also asked to consider how they will join the pieces of fabric together, how they will fasten it and how they may personalise it.

Activity sheet 'Make and use a pattern 2: backpacks' encourages students to look at backpacks in relation to the key terms: **fabric strength**, **durability**, **cost**, **fit for purpose**, **attractiveness** and **fastenings** and to identify solutions to each of the questions about making a backpack. Provide a range of backpacks from simple P.E. bags to backpacks manufactured for this purpose. Instruct students to focus on the handles or straps for carrying the backpack. Use your knowledge of the students' skills to influence them into choosing solutions that will enable them to make their backpack.

Plenary

Encourage discussion about the finished products made in this unit and invite students to comment on the difficulties that they may have encountered if they had not used a pattern.

Terms and symbols used on patterns

☞ Read these explanations of terms that you will see printed on patterns:

Stitching line. This is marked with a broken line, a small distance from the cutting line. This is the line that your stitches will go on.

Cutting line. The line to cut out on. It is shown as a solid line.

Seam allowance. The stitching line is shown as a dotted line, it is inside the cutting line so you can sew the fabric pieces.

Notches. These are marks on the cutting lines. Cut around them help you to sew the right pieces together.

Grain line. This is marked on the pattern by a line and by words. It is important to put the pattern pieces down the right way.

Centre front (or back). Don't cut or stitch on this line. It helps you to put everything together.

Fold line. Some pattern pieces go on a fold so that you cut out one piece. You put the solid line on the fabric fold.

Remember...

The pattern will tell you what you will need to cut out. It will tell you which types of fabric to buy and how much you will need.

Textiles

Pattern markings

This table lists the names of each of the markings you can see on the resource sheet 'Terms and symbols used on patterns'.

☞ Draw each one in the spaces in the table.

Name of the marking	Draw the marking here
Grain line	
Notches	
Cutting line	
Stitching line	
Fold line	

☞ These diagrams show patterns with markings on them. Write down the names of each marking that you can see. The words in the table will help you.

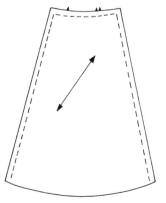
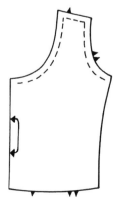

A pattern to make a glove puppet

☞ Use this sheet to help you to make a glove puppet. First, test the size of the pattern given to you by your teacher by placing your hand on it. Your hand must fit inside the stitching line with a space around it. Now, use these instructions to help you to make your puppet.

1. Fold your fabric in half.	
2. Look for the **selvages**. These are edges with a special finish. Place the pattern on so that the **grain line** marking is the same as the picture.	'grain line'
3. Pin the pattern on and cut out the pieces.	
4. Remove the pattern. Write your name on the fabric in pencil.	
5. Stitch the fabric together along the stitching line. Leave the bottom edge open. Stitch on top of the first row of stitches to make these stitches stronger.	
6. Carefully clip the seam allowances. Turn the puppet so that the seams are on the inside. Iron it flat and check that your hand fits inside.	
7. Decorate your puppet. Draw a face and hands on it or colour it with fabric crayons. You could also use buttons, beads or sequins.	

Textiles

Make and use a pattern 1: pencil case

☞ This pattern is for a pencil case. Read these steps and think about what you will need to consider to make a pencil case. Then, use the steps to make your pencil case.

1. What do you want to put in your pencil case? Measure the sizes of the things that you want to put into the case. Decide what length and how wide the case should be.	
2. Make a pattern for your pencil case. Use squared paper to draw it. Remember to draw the **cutting line** 1.5cm outside the **stitching line**. Draw on a **grain line**.	
3. Decide how you will close the case. Do you need to add a flap to close it? Draw a pattern for this.	
4. How will you hold the case shut? Mark where the fastenings will go.	
5. Choose a suitable fabric for your pencil case. Pin the pattern on and cut out the pieces.	
6. Join the pieces together and add your fastener.	
7. Put your pens and pencils in and try it out!	

Make and use a pattern 2: backpacks

☞ This sheet will help you to draw a pattern and to make a backpack. Read each of these steps and think about what you will need to make your backpack. Then, follow the steps to make your backpack.

1. Look at some backpacks. How many parts to the backpack are there? Draw a pattern for your backpack on squared paper. Remember to draw the **cutting line** 1.5cm from the **stitching line**. Draw the **grain line**.	*stitching line* / *grain line*
2. What are you going to put in your backpack? How big must it be?	
3. How will you close the bag? Will you pull a cord or do you need to add a flap to close it? Add these to your pattern.	
4. How will you neaten the edges?	
5. How will you keep it shut? Add your fastening to your pattern.	
6. How will you carry it? Do you need to make a handle? If you want to make straps, measure how long they should be and make a pattern for them.	
7. Choose a suitable fabric for your bag. Pin the pattern on, with the grain lines going the right way, and cut out the pieces.	
8. Sew the pieces together.	

Teacher's notes

Modelling and making toiles

Objectives

- To make a pattern from an existing product
- To know what the terms **modelling**, **prototyping** and **a toile** mean
- To use the computer to help model ideas, for example, colour ways

Prior knowledge

Students need to be able to cut out fabric accurately. They should know how to use a sewing machine to stitch and neaten a seam. Students will also need to be able to use a drawing package to complete activity sheet 'Modelling using a computer'.

QCA links

Unit 7biii Designing and making for yourself
Focus: textiles

NC links

Developing , planning, and communicating ideas: 1h. Working with tools, equipment, materials and components to produce quality products:2a, 2b, Breadth of study 7a, 7b,

Scottish attainment targets

Environmental Studies – Technology – Knowledge & Understanding: Strand – Needs and how they are met: Level D
Environmental Studies – Skills in Technology – designing and making: Strand – Preparing for tasks: Level D

Wales links

3.1   3.2

Northern Ireland links

Knowledge & understanding – Manufacturing materials, components, techniques and processes

Background

This unit covers making a pattern from an existing product (this could be any product depending on the interest of the students). Activity sheet 'Modelling a notebook cover' looks at testing any pattern by making up or modelling as well as creating a **toile** or **prototype** product. From experience modelling, producing a **toile** or **prototyping** is best carried out with a similar fabric to the final version J-cloths, or old t-shirts or recycled men's shirts are useful for this activity). Use knitted fabric if the product needs to be stretched to fit or use woven fabric where little movement is required.

Starter activity

Provide students with a J-cloth, scissors and a stapler. Ask them to make a simple container or a fun child's party hat from the resources you have provided. Alternatively, students could observe whilst you make a simple container or party hat. Either activity will lead into talking about modelling and why it is such an important activity when designing and making products.

Resource and activity sheets

The resource sheet 'Modelling toiles and prototypes' provides a visual example of a toile in use. This visual provides a reason for making a toile. Activity sheet 'Patterns' encourages students to make a pattern from an existing product. This activity sheet can be used with any product depending on what you are focusing on, for example, a t-shirt, a hat, a tie or a textile product like a wallet or a pencil case. Activity sheet 'Modelling a notebook cover' gives students step by step instructions for modelling a cover for a notebook.

Activity sheet 'Modelling using a computer' involves using a computer to help students to decide on a suitable colour scheme for a product. It could be completed as a focus practical task to teach students about seam allowances and additional fabric for movement. Activity sheet 'Taking measurements' is about taking into consideration what measurements need to be taken to make a variety of products. Be careful if looking at measuring students for making garments as this can be a sensitive area.

Plenary

Prepare for the plenary by producing a display table, for example, laying a table cloth over a table and place boxes underneath the cloth to provide some height to the display. Organise students to place their results from this unit onto the display table. Use the display as a focus for discussing the learning that has taken place during each activity.

Modelling toiles and prototypes

Making a product in cheap fabric before you make it for 'real' is called modelling.

The partly finished item is referred to as a **toile** or a **prototype**.

This allows you to check that the product is the correct size, style and shape.

A toile

This toile is **modelled** inside out. This makes alterations easier to do.

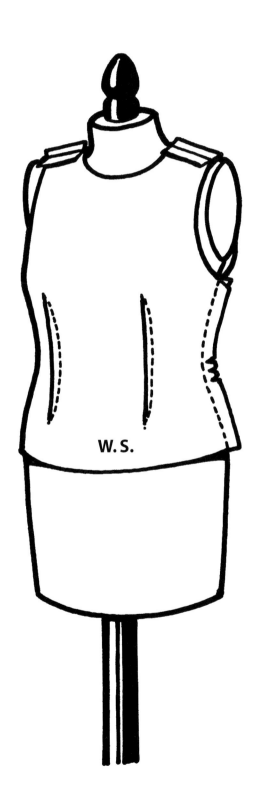

W. S.

Textiles

Activity sheet – Modelling and making toiles

Patterns

Patterns can be made from existing garments.

Garments are undone to find out the exact shape of fabric pieces needed to make the garment.

☞ Follow these steps to make a pattern from an existing garment.

1. Take a garment, for example, a t-shirt, a hat, or a tie.	
2. Undo all the stitches using a quick-un-pick. Go slowly so you don't accidentally cut the fabric shapes.	
3. The fabric shapes are the **pattern pieces** for the new product.	sleeve · back · front · neckband
4. Place the **pattern pieces** (fabric shapes) onto the new fabric and pin them in place. R.S. respresents **Right Side** of fabric.	R. S.
5. Carefully cut out the fabric exactly the same size as the **pattern pieces**.	
6. Stitch the new fabric shapes back together to make the new product.	

Modelling a notebook cover

☞ Use this sheet to help you to make a notebook cover. You teacher will help you with any words you are unsure of.

What you will need:

- newspaper for the pattern
- a notebook to cover
- sewing thread
- low-cost fabric, for example, a J-cloth
- a sewing machine
- pins

What you need to do:

1.	Place a tape measure around the notebook from front to back. Then, add 10cm to this measurement.	
2.	Measure the height of the notebook. Then, add 6cm to this measurement.	
3.	Cut a pattern to these measurements from newspaper or scrap paper.	
4.	Pin the pattern down onto the fabric and cut out the fabric.	
5.	Neaten the edges of the fabric with a zig-zag machine stitch.	
6.	Pin the fabric in place around the book. Draw a line across the top and bottom edges of the notebook. Machine across this line.	
7.	Turn the flaps through to the right side of the fabric.	
8.	Put the cover onto the book using the flaps to hold the cover in place.	

Textiles

Activity sheet – Modelling and making toiles

Modelling using a computer

☞ Use this sheet to help you to carry out modelling using a computer.

What you will need:

- a computer
- drawing software package
- a printer

What you will need to do:

1. On the computer, draw a simple rectangular pencil case with a zip on the top edge and a motif on the front.

2. Copy and paste this sketch several times on your computer screen.

3. Use colour to 'fill in' the pencil cases and the motifs.

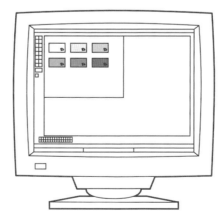

4. Modelling your pencil case will help you to decide which colours you like the best.

Textiles

Activity sheet – Modelling and making toiles

Taking measurements

A tape measure is used to measure curved items, for example, the body because it is bendy.

☞ Use this diagram to help you to answer the questions below.

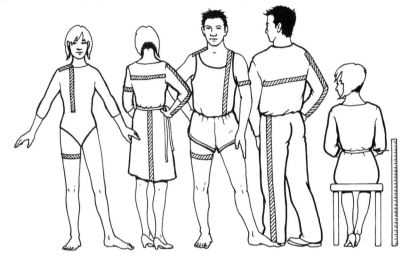

☞ Draw on the picture below where you think you would measure.

1. What measurements do you need to make a t-shirt?

2. What measurements will you need to make a pair of trousers?

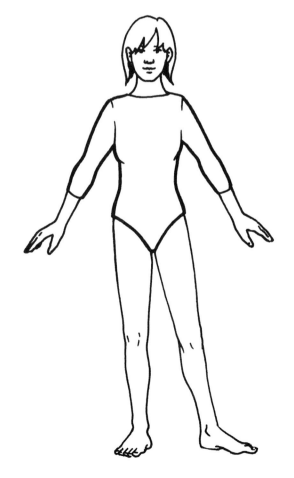

Textiles

Teacher's notes

Equipment

Objectives

- To be able to select the correct equipment for the task
- To know the names of different pieces of equipment
- To be able to use small equipment with confidence

Prior knowledge

Some knowledge about small pieces of equipment would be helpful. The ability to use a sewing machine is also advisable but not essential for activity sheet 'Selecting and using equipment to make a quilted card'. However, a sewing machine will be necessary for activity sheet 'Making a fabric tag'.

QCA links

Unit 7e Activity week (optional) Focus: textiles
Unit 7b iii Designing and making for yourself
Focus: textiles

NC links

Working with tools, equipment, materials and components to produce quality products: 2a, 2c, 2d.

Scottish attainment targets

Environmental Studies – Technology – Knowledge & Understanding: Strand – Processes and how they are applied: Level D
Environmental Studies – Skills in Technology – designing and making: Strand – Carrying out tasks: Level D

Wales links

5.1

Northern Ireland links

Knowledge & understanding – Manufacturing materials, components, techniques and processes

Background

This unit is about the small equipment needed when working with fabrics and threads. The two products covered (an ID tag and a quilted card) encourage students to work with the equipment. The activity sheets would work best when accompanied by an actual or photographed equipment display with labels to say what each piece of equipment is used for.

Starter activity

Create a display of the small equipment before the students arrive in the class. Ask them to think about what the equipment might be used for and its cost. Encourage students to guess the price of the equipment. Ask the student whose answer is the nearest to the correct price to write a price label and to place it on the display.

Resource and activity sheets

The resource sheet 'Choosing equipment' shows sketches of the pieces of small equipment. When referring to these, teachers should note that they would work best when accompanied by a display of small equipment complete with clear labels about what the pieces of are used for. Activity sheets 'Selecting and using equipment to make a quilted card' (1) and (2) show students how they could make a quilted card. Students can complete this activity with hand or machine stitches depending on their ability. Point out to students that whilst you can use sewing thread for either hand or machine stitches, hand stitches would look better with an embroidery thread such as soft embroidery or perle thread. Students should also note that sewing machine stitches or patterns would look at their best if machine embroidery thread is used on the machine.

Students should then use what they have learned to help them to complete the final activity 'Making a fabric tag'. Read through the steps with students and any terms which they need guidance on before asking them to make their ID tags.

Plenary

Place the pieces of small equipment into a bag. Ask a student to take a piece of equipment very carefully from the bag. The student can then name the piece of equipment and say what they might use it for. This should repeated around the classroom until all the pieces of equipment are removed from the bag.

You could ask students to give each piece of equipment a mark out of 10 based on the following factors: *Which piece of equipment is their favourite piece? Why? Which piece of equipment is the easiest to use? Why?* And so on.

Choosing equipment

Equipment name		What is it used for?
Embroidery frame		An embroidery frame is used to hold fabric.
Fabric marker or pen		A fabric marker or pen is used to mark the fabric, so you know where to stitch.
Needles		Needles are used to stitch fabrics together.
Pins		Pins are used to hold fabrics together.
Tape measure		A tape measure is used to measure fabrics. It will bend easily.
Scissors		Scissors are used to cut fabric and threads.
Sewing thread		Sewing thread is used to hold fabrics together.
Sewing machine		A sewing machine is used to stitch fabrics together.
Quick-un-pick		A quick-un-pick is used to undo stitches.

Selecting and using equipment to make a quilted card (1)

☞ This sheet shows you how to make a quilted card.

What you will need

- fabric (for the top layer)
- wadding (for the middle layer)
- backing fabric (for the bottom layer)
- pins

- a needle
- sewing thread
- card mount
- a sewing machine (optional)

What you will need to do :

☞ Follow these steps to make a quilted card. You will need to fill in the missing words to help you.

1. Take the three fabric layers and hold them together with	
2. Tacking stitches are large straight stitches. Tack all the layers together using a .... and sewing thread.	
3. Using a .... draw a simple pattern on the top layer of the fabric sandwich.	

Selecting and using equipment to make a quilted card (2)

4. Follow the lines you have drawn on the fabric. Start in the middle and stitch the fabric layers together. Use either a .... or hand stitches.	
5. Remove the tacking stitches using a	
6. Cut off any loose threads using	
7. Stick the quilted design onto the card mount. (Use the diagram below to show you how to stick the quilted design in the correct place).	
8. You now have a quilted card.	

Word bank			
pins	needle	fabric marker or pen	sewing machine

Health and safety points

- When using pins and needles, don't hurt yourself.
- When using the sewing machine:
    - keep your fingers away from the needle;
    - put the presser foot down;
    - tie back long hair.
- Don't cut yourself when using a quick-un-pick or scissors.

Ask your teacher if you are unsure about anything!

Textiles

Activity sheet – Equipment

Making a fabric tag

☞ This activity sheet shows you how to make an ID Tag.

What you will need:

- denim
- an eyelet
- sewing thread
- fabric
- a sewing machine

What you will need to do: (Note that R.S. represents 'Right Side' of fabric. W.S. represents 'Wrong Side' of fabric.)

1. Cut out two pieces of fabric, 1.5cm larger all around than the size you would like your tag. This is the seam allowance.	R.S. R.S.
2. Put the two pieces of fabric together with the right sides of the fabric facing each other. Pin the fabric pieces together.	W.S.
3. Use large straight stitches to hold the fabrics together.	W.S.
4. Machine around the shape, but leave a gap.	W.S.
5. Trim down the seam allowance and cut off the corners.	W.S.
6. Turn the fabric through the gap to show the right side of the fabric.	R.S.
7. Machine around the edge of the tag.	R.S.
8. Put an eyelet into the tag. Add the name you want to appear on the tag with glitter glue.	julie

Teacher's notes

Colouring fabrics with dyes and crayons

Objectives

- To know the different ways to add colour to fabrics
- To know and understand the vocabulary connected with the different processes
- To be able to work independently
- To be able to be creative and imaginative in producing samples

Prior knowledge

Students will need to be able to follow written instructions and have some knowledge about colour. They must be strong enough to tie string and wind elastic bands around the fabric.

QCA links

Unit 7aiii Understanding materials Focus: textiles
Unit 7e Activity week Focus: textiles
Un it 8biii Designing for clients Focus: textiles
Unit 8aiii Exploring materials Focus: textiles

NC links

Knowledge and understanding of materials and components 4c, Working with tools, equipment, materials, and components to produce quality products 2a, Breadth of study 7b

Scottish attainment targets

Environmental Studies – Technology – Knowledge & Understanding: Strand – Resources and how they are managed: Level D
Strand – Processes and how they are applied: Level D
Environmental Studies – Skills in Technology – designing and making: Strand – Carrying out tasks: Level C

Wales links

3.1   3.2

Northern Ireland links

Knowledge & understanding – Manufacturing materials, components, techniques and processes

Background

This unit provides tasks to develop students' skills in making design decisions about how colour can be added to a textile product.

Students are given step-by-step instructions of how to create a sample of tie dye, block printing, stencilling and fabric crayons. Note that natural fibres work best for tie dye and block printing work, for example, cotton, calico. Fabric crayons often work well on synthetic fibre fabrics, for example, 100% polyester satin. However, this will very much depend on the type of crayons which are used. Crayons can be **waxy** or can be **felt-tipped** and come in a range of colours.

Starter activity

Provide students with a selection of samples of technique and labels for the different processes they will be studying throughout this unit. Students should match the labels to the techniques.

Resource and activity sheets

Provide students with either samples or good quality photographs of each of the processes covered during this unit. **Dye baths**, **dye pads** and **printing pads** should be made available. Students should study the resource sheet 'Colouring fabrics', which provides them with some information about each of the processes they will cover during this unit. Read through each of the processes with students, encouraging them to give examples of products which have been made using each of the processes.

Students should then work through the activity sheets provided which give step-by-step instructions for carrying out each of the processes. When completing activity sheet 'Tie dye' explain to students that a **dye bath** is a plastic or glass container which holds the liquid dye. Students should also be aware of the term **dye pad** when completing activity sheet 'Block printing'. This is a 'pad' soaked in thick dye. The pad can be made from sponge or felt and placed onto a hard surface, for example, a plate. The dye used for a dye pad is thick. Activity sheet 'Using fabric crayons' looks at the use of a **printing pad** – smooth newsprint paper on a desk/table will produce a smooth printing surface.

Plenary

Explain the different steps involved in the various techniques used in this unit, recapping the processes using question and answer processes. Students could then be selected or volunteered to stand in a line (the same number of students as steps to a specific process). Students should then explain the steps in the process.

Always monitor students using dyes, irons and other equipment.

Colouring fabrics

Tie dye

Tie dye is where the fabric is tied up and then dyed. The dye reaches the fabric that isn't tied. Fabrics can be tied and dyed a number of different times to create some exciting patterns.

Block printing

The printing block is pressed onto a **dye pad** and then pressed onto the fabric. A print is then left on the fabric.

 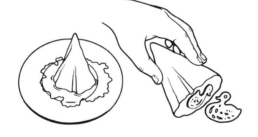 

Stencilling

First, a stencil needs to be made. The stencil is placed on the fabric. Dye is then sponged through the holes in the stencil.

Fabric crayons

There are a number of different types of crayons. They all come in a wide range of colours. These are easy to use. Crayon directly onto the fabric, enlarge areas or just draw lines.

Textiles

Tie dye

☞ This activity sheet shows you how to **tie dye** a piece of fabric.

What you will need:

- natural fabric
- string, elastic bands or pegs
- dye bath

What you will need to do:

1. Tie the fabric up really tightly using cotton, string, elastic bands or pegs. **Remember the fabric must be tied very tight!**	
2. Wet the fabric. Place it in the dye bath for one hour.	
3. Take the fabric out of the dye bath. Rinse the fabric under a cold tap, until the water runs clear.	
4. Untie your fabric and leave it to dry.	
5. Iron your fabric to remove the creases.	

Health and safety

- Use rubber gloves when using the dye bath.
- Take care not to burn yourself when using the iron.

Activity sheet – Colouring fabrics with dyes and crayons

Block printing

☞ This activity sheet shows you how to use block printing.

What you will need:

- a printing block
- a dye pad
- a printing pad (a few sheets of flat newspaper)
- natural fabric
- masking tape

What you will need to do:

1. Take a printing block.	
2. Use masking tape to stick the fabric on top of a pad of flat newspaper on a table. Press the block into the dye pad and then press the block onto the fabric.	
3. A print of the raise pattern should appear on the fabric.	
4. Print your block in this pattern.	
5. Now, print your block in this pattern. Your teacher will provide you with a full-size version.	

☞ Can you think of any other ways to arrange your printing block to create a pattern?

Activity sheet – Colouring fabrics with dyes and crayons

Using fabric crayons

Fabric crayons can be used to create outlines and to fill in shapes with colour.

☞ This activity sheet shows you how to add colour to fabric using crayons.

What you will need:

- fabric crayons
- fabric
- printing pad
- masking tape

What you will need to do:

Follow these steps:	These drawings will help you.
1. Use the masking tape to stick the fabric on top of the printing pad. (The fabric must be very tight to draw on.)	3.
2. Choose a letter.	
3. Draw an outline of the letter on to the fabric using the crayons.	4.
4. Draw the same letter again, but make the letter larger.	
5. Draw the same letter again, but make the letter smaller.	7.
6. Draw the same letter again and again. Change the size and overlap the letters to create a random letter pattern.	
7. Colour in the shapes which have been created by the overlapping letters.	

Activity sheet – Colouring fabrics with dyes and crayons

Stencilling

What you will need:

- sticky backed plastic (book covering)
- thick fabric printing dye
- masking tape
- a cutting mat
- fabric, for example, cotton or calico
- a printing pad
- a craft knife
- a sponge

Health and safety
When using a craft knife:
- use a cutting mat; • tighten the blade in the craft knife; • keep your fingers away from the cutting blade; • use a metal ruler when cutting a straight line.

What you will need to do:

Follow these steps:	Use these drawings to help you.
1. Draw a shape on the 'paper' side of the sticky backed plastic, for example, a flower.	**1.**
2. Use the craft knife and a cutting mat to cut out the shape. (Keep the **cut-out shape** and the **shape with a hole** in the middle.)	**2.**
3. Use masking tape to stick the fabric onto the top of the printing pad.	
4. Press the sticky backed plastic with **a hole in it** (the stencil) on to the fabric.	**5.**
5. Using a **dye pad**, carefully dab the dye coated sponge over the stencil onto the fabric.	
6. Lift off the sticky backed plastic. You have created a **positive shape**.	**6.**

 You should hold the craft knife parallel to the sticky backed plastic to cut out the shape easily.

Teacher's notes

Embellishment

Objectives

- To be aware of manufactured fabrics, which are embellished as part of their production
- To be able to follow simple instructions to understand the technique of appliqué
- To learn about the technique of quilting and practise it
- To know about and have practised with a few basic embroidery stitches
- To be able to use some of the skills learned in this unit and understand law to add items to further embellish an end product

Prior knowledge

Unit 8aiii Exploring materials Focus: textiles

QCA links

Knowledge and understanding of materials and components – 4c – that materials and components can be combined, processed & finished to create particular aesthetic effects.

NC links

KS3 Scheme of Work Unit 8A Finding an Identity and Unit 8C t-shirt challenge

Scottish attainment targets

Environmental Studies – Technology – Knowledge & Understanding: Strand – Needs and how they are met: Level D
Strand – Resources and how they are managed: Level D
Strand – Processes and how they are applied: Level D
Environmental Studies – Skills in Technology – designing and making: Strand – Carrying out tasks: Level C

Wales links

3.1   5.2   5.5

Northern Ireland links

Knowledge & understanding – Manufacturing materials, components, techniques and processes

Background

Students who find it difficult to manipulate fabrics, may achieve better results in this unit if you encourage them to work with coloured felt.

It is suggested that iron-on fusible interfacing, for example, Bondaweb is used to make the appliqué technique easier. The appliqué is fused onto the base fabric and further sewing is not essential, but it is easier for students to learn how to sew on this type of base. If possible, provide embroidery hoops to hold and stretch the fabric out as this will help students to manipulate the materials more successfully.

Starter activity

Provide each of the students with a piece of fabric that has a design printed on it, for example, the outline of an animal. Ask them to suggest ways of making the design more interesting and then allow them to glue items on to the outlines. Encourage students to understand that to be **fit for purpose**, an embellishment must stand up to normal use.

Resource and activity sheets

The resource sheet 'Embellishment' describes to students how some fabrics have been made more attractive during their manufacture. It also defines the techniques they will experience during this unit.

Activity sheet 'Applique' describes the technique of appliqué and a simple way of achieving it. This technique is good for applying reflective strips to bags and badges.

The activity sheet 'Quilting' describes the quilting process and suggests a very simple way to use it to produce a decorative panel or a motif. Make sure that the fabric is quilted before it is cut to make a product. A selection of fabric remnants with simple, bold designs should be collected before this activity is started. Explain to students that specially printed cotton fabric can be purchased which has suitable designs for quilting or appliqué on it.

The activity sheet 'Embroidery' describes to students three embroidery stitches. The stitches should be worked on felt, so that it is easy to handle, and finished shapes can be used to make products. Students will need to be taught how many strands of embroidery thread to use. When completing activity sheet 'Adding sequins, beads and buttons', students should follow the instructions to add sequins, beads or buttons to existing designs.

Plenary

Ask students to discuss the techniques used during this unit and the problems that they encountered.

Embellishment

A fabric looks the way it does because of the way it was made. You can add things to fabric before you use it.

☞ This sheet tells you about some of the words you will use in this unit.

- **Embellishment**   something added to the fabric
- **Appliqué**   a way of sewing a shape onto fabric
- **Quilting**   fabrics sewn together with wadding between the layers
- **Embroidery**   stitches to decorate
- **Fusible interfacing**   bonds fabrics together with the heat of an iron
- **Running stitch**   easy in and out stitch
- **Chain stitch**   stitches which look like a chain
- **Lazy daisy stitch**   stitches which look like a flower petal

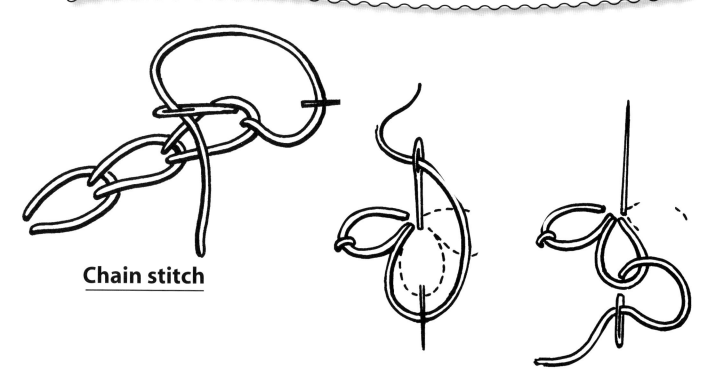

Chain stitch

Lazy daisy stitch

Appliqué

Appliqué is a **shape** put onto fabric before you start to a make a product.

Follow the steps below. You will need to use felt and iron-on fusible interfacing. Use resource sheet 'Embellishment' to help you.

1. Choose a shape.	
2. Cut it out of card.	
3. Choose a piece of felt big enough to fit the shape.	
4. Cut out the felt shape and the iron-on fusible interfacing.	
5. Iron the shape onto a background fabric (check with your teacher).	
6. Sew the shape down with a **running stitch**.	

☞ You may have ideas about using appliqué. For example, it would have been a good **technique** to use to make a safety badge. Can you think of some others?

Activity sheet – Embellishment

Quilting

Quilting is putting **wadding** between two layers of fabric to pad them. Quilted fabrics look pretty and are warm.

☞ Follow the steps below.

What you will need to do:

1.	Choose fabric with a **shape** on that you like, for example, a flower. Cut out a rectangle of the fabric with the shape in the centre.
2.	Cut out backing fabric and wadding the same size.
3.	Pin all the fabrics together.
4.	Sew around the shape. Either use a **running stitch** or a sewing machine. Go through all the layers.
5.	Use a zig-zag stitch to neaten the edges of the rectangle.

Using the quilted shape

☞ Use your quilted shape to make a greeting card.

1.	Choose a piece of card.
2.	Fold it in half.
3.	Use double-sided tape to stick your shape onto the card.
4.	Write a greeting on the front and the inside.

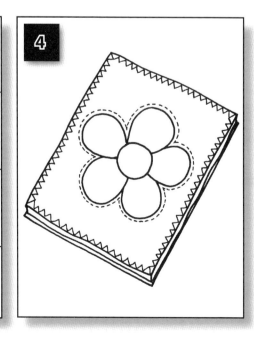

Textiles

Activity sheet – Embellishment

Embroidery

☞ This sheet shows you how to sew a **running stitch**, **chain stitch** and **lazy daisy stitch**. Follow the steps below.

You will need:

- a needle
- felt
- **embroidery** thread
- a pencil or chalk
- scissors

Running stitch

1. Draw a shape on the felt using a pencil or chalk.	1.
2. Sew running stitches around your shape by putting the needle in and out of the felt.	2.

Chain stitch

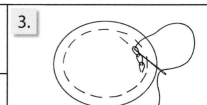

3. Around the inside of the running stitch, sew a chain stitch. Push the needle up and pull the thread through.	3.
4. Put the needle back into the place where the thread is coming out and then up and loop the thread under the needle.	4.
5. Pull gently to close the loop and then make another stitch the same.	

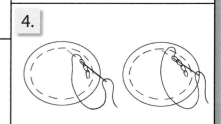

Lazy daisy stitch

6. When you have gone round the running stitch, make single looped stitches outside the running stitches. These are **lazy daisy** stitches.	5.

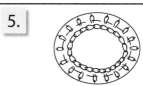

☞ Now you have **embroidered** one piece of felt. Try again on another piece. Keep all of the pieces.

Activity sheet – Embellishment

Adding sequins, beads and buttons

☞ This activity sheet shows you how to add **sequins, beads** or **buttons** to a shape. Follow the steps below.

What you will need:

- a selection of sequins, beads and buttons
- glue
- a piece of felt
- a needle and thread

What you will need to do:

Sewing on a **sequin**

- Choose where you want the sequin to be.
- Push the needle through the felt and into the hole of the sequin.
- Pull the thread through and put the needle back into the felt.
- Pull the thread through and then make another stitch through the sequin and pull it tight.

Sewing on a **bead**

- Put the needle through the felt and put a bead onto the needle.
- Pull gently, then put the needle back into the felt near to where the thread is already coming through.

Sewing on a **button**

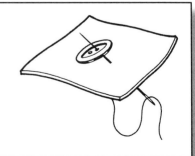

- Use the holes in the button to put the needle through.
- Sew four stitches on top of each other to hold the button on.
- Finish the stitches at the back of the felt.

Teacher's notes

Joining and finishing

Objectives

- To be able to join two pieces of fabric together
- To understand what a flat seam is
- To be able to choose the best way to neaten the edges of a flat seam
- To be able to set the sewing machine to machine straight stitch and zig-zag stitch

Prior knowledge

Students need to be able to use a sewing machine independently. They should also be able to machine in a straight line, measure accurately and turn a corner.

QCA links

Unit 7biii Designing and making for yourself Focus: textiles
Unit 6 Transition: building on learning from key stage 2 Focus: textiles

NC links

Knowledge and understanding of materials and components: 4c

Scottish attainment targets

Environmental Studies – Technology – Knowledge & Understanding
Strand – Needs and how they are met: Level D
Environmental Studies – Skills in Technology – designing and making
Strand – Carrying out tasks: Level E
Strand – Reviewing and reporting on tasks: Level E

Wales links

3.1   3.2

Northern Ireland links

Knowledge & understanding – Manufacturing materials, components, techniques and processes

refers to neatening the fraying edges of a product, as well as cutting off any **ends** of sewing thread and pressing the product to ensure that it looks good. A well finished product can be described as a product which one would sell in a shop.

Starter activity

Provide students with garments which show how different garments have been joined together as well as how edges have been finished.

Resource and activity sheets

Students may find it useful to refer to the garments provided in the starter activity to help them during this unit. Students should also bring in their own choice of top, jacket, skirt or trousers for reference.

The resource sheet 'Joining and finishing' provides students with a preview of the vocabulary which will be used when making and neatening a seam. Students should then use the activity sheets which follow, 'Joining fabrics together', 'Choosing seams and finishing techniques' and 'Hems' to learn the processes used to join fabrics together. For each of the activity sheets listed, teachers should first demonstrate each of the steps provided. The sheets should then be used as a learning support for students following the demonstrations. You may wish to enlarge each of the activity sheets to A3 size if students are having difficulty following the steps.

Students should use activity sheet 'Making a simple pencil case' to practice seams. This activity also shows students how to attach Velcro.

Plenary

Place each of the students' names into a bag at the beginning of the lesson. At the end of the lesson, pull a name out of the bag one by one. The student whose name is pulled from the bag should explain a step in the making of a seam or of a hem. You could also photocopy the three activity sheets which look at seams and hems and cut them up, asking students to put them back together, placing the sets in the correct order. Students could work in pairs to complete this activity.

Background

This unit covers the basics of joining fabric together and how to deal with frayed edges, for example, how to create a hem. Students will also learn about 'finishing a product'. Ensure students understand that **finishing**

Joining and finishing

Fabrics are joined together with seams. The most common seam is called a **flat seam**.

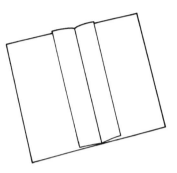

A flat seam can be neatened in different ways.

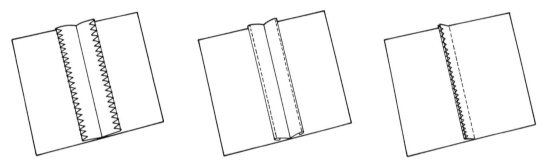

A seam can also be created using an overlocker machine. This machine will stitch, trim and neaten a seam in one process. This process is often used by industry.

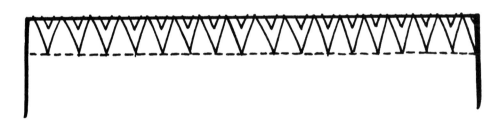

Finishing fabrics

Fraying edges of fabric are often neatened with a hem.

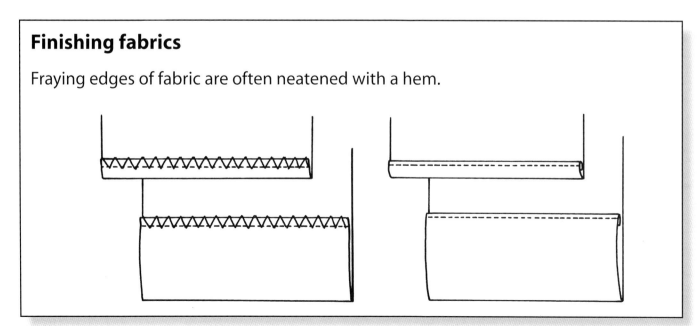

Activity sheet – Joining and finishing

Joining fabrics together

☞ These steps will show you how to make a flat seam.

1. Pin the two edges together.

2. Tack the pieces of fabric together.

3. Remove the pins. Machine along the tacking line.

4. Remove the tacking stitches.

☞ There are two ways of neatening the edges. Select one way to neaten the edges.

Method 1

1. Neaten each edge of the seam with a zig-zag stitch.

2. Press the seam flat.

Method 2

1. Trim the seam down to 7.5mm.

2. Zig-zag both pieces of fabric together.

3. Press the seam to one side.

Choosing seams and finishing techniques

☞ Complete this table.

Seam and finish	Draw a garment for the seam

Activity sheet – Joining and finishing

Hems

☞ This sheet shows you how to create a hem.

Hem method 1

1. Turn under 1/2cm of fabric and then another 1/2cm of fabric. Press the hem into place.	
2. Pin the hem.	Pinned 5mm
3. Tack the hem.	Tacked 5mm pinned
4. Machine the hem using a straight or zig-zag stitch.	

Hem method 2

1. Zig-zag over the fraying edges.	
2. Fold over 1/2cm of the neatened edge of fabric to make a hem and press it into place.	
3. Pin and tack the hem in place.	Pinned
4. Machine the hem in place using a straight stitch on top of the zig-zag stitches.	

Note...

You can change the width of the hem.

Activity sheet – Joining and finishing

Making a simple pencil case

☞ Use this sheet to practice what you have learned to make a pencil case.

What you will need:

- two pieces of fabric (they should be exactly the same size)
- sewing thread
- one piece of Velcro

What you will need to do:

1. Place the two pieces of fabric together.	
2. Machine the two pieces of fabric together. Make sure you leave a gap.	
3. Trim down the seam allowance.	
4. Turn the fabric through.	
5. Press the fabric so that the seam is on the edge.	
6. Put the seam allowance into the gap. Machine around the edge of the fabric.	
7. Pin and tack the Velcro in place.	
8. Machine around the Velcro.	
9. Fold the fabric up to create a 'pocket'. Machine down the edges to hold the 'pocket' in place.	
10. Now, fold over the top of the edge to make your pencil case!	

Teacher's notes

Testing

Objectives

- To be able to complete simple fabric tests
- To be able to evaluate results from the fabric tests
- To be able to match a fabric test against a property required of the finished product
- To know how to evaluate a finished product
- To understand the relevant vocabulary involved in testing fabrics

Prior knowledge

Students need to understand how fabrics are constructed from fibres, which are either made into a yarn and then knitted, or woven together to make a fabric. They should also understand key words such as **absorbent**, **washability**, **wear resistant**, **stretchy** and so on.

QCA links

Unit 7aiii Understanding materials Focus: textiles
Unit 9aiii Selecting materials
Focus: textiles

NC links

Developing planning and communicating ideas 1a, Evaluating processes and products 3a, 3c

Scottish attainment targets

Environmental Studies – Technology – Knowledge & Understanding: Strand – Resources and how they are managed: Level E
Strand – Processes and how they are applied: Level E
Environmental Studies – Skills in Technology – designing and making: Strand – Carrying out tasks: Level E
Strand – Reviewing and reporting on tasks: Level D, Level E

Wales links

3.1   5.7

Northern Ireland links

Knowledge & understanding – Manufacturing materials, components, techniques and processes

Background

This unit looks at some simple tests for various properties of fabrics. Use this unit to teach students how to carry out basic tests on fabrics to find out their properties.

Starter activity

The starter activity looks at sorting and exploring fabrics. Provide students with a selection of fabric samples to look at, to hold, to stretch and to generally explore. Use up to 20 pieces of fabric. Students could discuss the properties of each in groups. Ask them to consider these questions: *Which fabrics feel good? Which fabrics are natural? Which fabrics are woven? Which fabrics are knitted?*

Resource and activity sheets

The resource sheet 'Testing' gives students information about fabric testing. This sheet should be used in conjunction with the activity sheets.

Activity sheet 'Matching the fabric test to the product' asks students to consider what tests would have been carried out on the fabric used to make each of the products shown.

Students should then move onto activity sheet 'Researching information about a product' which provides a simple way of analysing a product by completing a star chart and creating a product profile.

Activity sheet 'Finding out about a fabric' asks students to look closely at a fabric and to write a simple fabric specification. A template has been provided.

The final activity sheet 'Analysing a textile product' can be used to evaluate any textile product. First, show students a variety of different products. The questions on the activity sheet are simple. Students should answer 'Yes' or 'No' and their answers should be shared orally with the class. This activity could be completed independently or in pairs.

Plenary

Ask students some key questions to check the learning that has taken place during this unit. You could ask students:

- *Why do we need to look closely at existing products before designing new ones?*
- *Why do we need to test fabrics before we use them to make new products?*
- *Why do we need to think about what the textile product must do before we choose a fabric?*

Testing

Property	The test	Description of the test
Absorbency How much water will the fabric absorb?		Add drops of water to the fabric. How many drops will the fabric absorb? Record the number of drops the fabric can absorb.
Washability Does the fabric change in colour or size when it is washed and dried lots of times?		Take two samples of fabric. Wash and dry one fabric sample several times. Does the washed fabric sample look the same as the original sample? Is it the same colour? Is it the same size? Record these results.
Wear resistance Does the fabric resist wear and tear?		Pin some glass paper onto a block of wood. Attach a sample of fabric to another block of wood. Rub the two blocks together. How many times can you rub the fabric before the fabric is bubbly, fluffy or holes appear?
Stretch Does the fabric return to the original size when stretched?		Take two pieces of fabric. Pull and stretch one sample of fabric. Is this sample different in size to the original sample? How stretchy is the fabric?

Activity sheet – Testing

Matching the fabric test to the product

☞ Decide which fabric tests you would choose for the following products?

Activity sheet – Testing

Researching information about a product

Your teacher will provide you with some textile products. Choose one. Look at it, hold it, use it and find out what it cost.

Record a mark out of five for each question on the star diagram below.

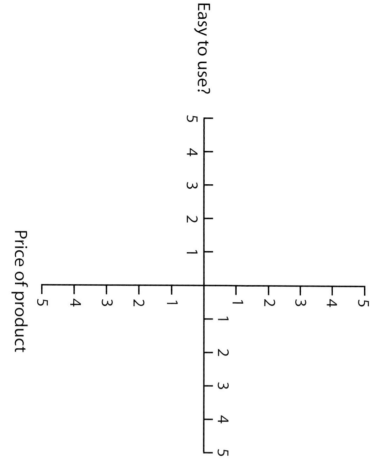

Easy to use?

Look of product

Price of product

Feel of fabric

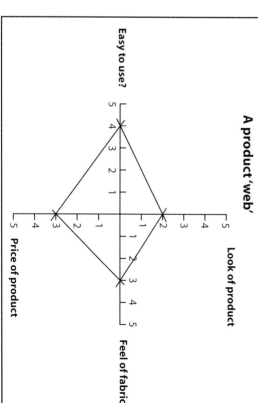

A product 'web'

Easy to use?

Look of product

Price of product

Feel of fabric

Now, join up your marks to create a product 'web'.

Finding out about a fabric

☞ Use this activity to help you to find out about any fabric.

Looking at the fabric	Questions	What have you found out about the fabric?
Use a magnifying glass to help you to look closely at the fabric. Describe what you can see.	● Is the fabric plain? ● How has the fabric been constructed?	The fabric is: ● .... ● .... ● ....
Touching the fabric Use your hands to hold, pull and scrunch the fabric. What happens?	● How does the fabric feel? ● How stretchy is the fabric? ● Does the fabric crease easily?	● .... ● .... ● ....

Word bank

woven   knitted   bonded   shiny   matt   soft   smooth   silky   rough   ribbed

Textiles

Activity sheet – Testing

Analysing a textile product

☞ Your teacher will show you some textile products. Look at each one and answer these questions. Colour the bars on the right of the question to record your answers to the questions.

You should then discuss why you have chosen 'Yes' or 'No' in groups.

	Yes	No

Do you like the look of the product?
Why?

....

....

Do you think the product is priced correctly?
Why?

....

....

Is the product easy to use?
Why?

....

....

Can the product do what it is supposed to do?
Why?

....

....

Has the correct fabric been used?
Why?

....

....

Is the product a **green** eco-friendly product?
Why?

....

....

Assessment sheet – Textiles

✓ Tick the boxes that show what you know.

I know:

	know / yes	not sure / sometimes	don't know / no
1 how to listen to the teacher			
2 how to work well with a partner			
3 how to work well in a group			
4			
5			
6			
7			
8			
9			
10			

I know best / I can do best:

_____

_____

I need to: (write no more than three targets.)

_____

_____

_____